Covered Bridges

Across North America

Joseph D. Conwill

Dedication
This book is dedicated to Richard Sanders Allen.

This edition first published in 2004 by MBI, an imprint of MBI Publishing Company, Galtier Plaza, Suite 200, 380 Jackson Street, St. Paul, MN 55101-3885 USA

The information in this book is true and complete to the best of our knowledge. All recommendations are made without any guarantee on the part of the author or Publisher, who also disclaim any liability incurred in connection with the use of this data or specific details.

We recognize that some words, model names and designations, for example, mentioned herein are the property of the trademark holder. We use them for identification purposes only. This is not an official publication.

MBI titles are also available at discounts in bulk quantity for industrial or sales-promotional use. For details write to Special Sales Manager at Motorbooks International Wholesalers & Distributors, Galtier Plaza, Suite 200, 380 Jackson Street, St. Paul, MN55101-3885 USA.

ISBN 0-7603-1822-0

Edited by Amy Glaser
Designed by LeAnn Kuhlmann
Printed in China

On the front cover: The covered bridge in Stark is said to be the most photographed in New Hampshire. Local officials had power lines buried underground to preserve this view.

On the frontispiece: Shryer Bridge has been removed from the public road system of Fairfield County, Ohio, since this photo was taken in 1977. It is now on private property near its original location.

On the title page: The West Hill Bridge in Montgomery, Vermont, is another authentic covered bridge, but it is not presently in service. The setting is among the most beautiful in New England, but the trees have grown considerably since 1974, when this view was captured, and the bridge is now almost completely hidden in foliage.

On the back cover, top: Gregg Bridge, over Wakatomika Creek in Licking County, Ohio, looked like an antique in 1973. It was built with the multiple kingpost truss, which is typical in this region. **Bottom:** This view, taken in 2002, shows Bath-Haverhill Bridge in need of restoration. Work is scheduled to begin soon.

CONTENTS

INTRODUCTION

A powerful symbol in America's rural past is the old covered bridge. It seems to promise all the best features of bygone country life: a cool fragrant wooden space like an old barn, built of hand-hewn timbers, beside sunny fields or quiet forests, over rolling waters. Despite the spread of suburbs and of heavy traffic far into the country, covered bridges still offer the expected image in many areas.

The history of these structures is not well understood. For one thing, they are not that rare. Some parts of America have none at all, and other regions only have a few. States such as Pennsylvania, Ohio, Vermont, Indiana, New Hampshire, and Oregon still have many covered bridges. Nationwide there are about 750 covered bridges, with

Pennsylvania has over 200 covered bridges, which is more than any other state. This example crosses Shermans Creek near New Germantown in Perry County.

another 150 in Canada. Their numbers are slowly declining, but they are still tourist destinations in much of North America.

That so many covered bridges survive is not an historical accident. They are still around because of their strong popular appeal. Methods of preserving them draw some debate, but no one has advocated their wholesale replacement since the mid-1960s. Today, three to eight per year are lost, sometimes because of floods or overloading, more often by arson, and occasionally because of misguided repairs.

Covered bridges were not always examples of rural charm. The first American examples dated from the first decade of the nineteenth century and were located on important travel routes, often in urban locations. A covered bridge was the engineering marvel of its day. By the time of the Civil War, the covered bridge had become a standard structure and attracted no more attention than a modern freeway overpass would today.

Shortly after 1900, steel bridges were the new standard, and covered wooden bridges saw their worst days in the eastern United States. They were useless eyesores, havens for idlers and thugs, obstacles to spartan progress, and plastered with unsightly advertising posters. Ironically, the same period saw the beginnings of a covered bridge construction boom elsewhere because scientific stress analysis made the old

Hectorville Bridge used to span South Branch Trout River in Montgomery, Vermont. The bridge has since been moved, and this 1974 view is of the original location.

Baker's Camp Bridge near Bainbridge in Putnam County, Indiana, still looked rustic in 1978. Most of the photographs in this book show the bridges as they looked before modern modifications such as steel guard rails.

Prather's Bridge crossed Tugaloo River on the state line between South Carolina and Georgia. Built in 1920, it was destroyed by arson in 1978. There are still three interstate covered bridges on the New Hampshire–Vermont state line.

designs more economical than ever in timber-rich regions such as Oregon, Quebec, and New Brunswick.

The devastating flood of 1927 took out huge numbers of covered bridges in New England, and the Midwest experienced a similar disaster in 1913. Earlier floods had caused big flurries of new covered bridge construction, but by the 1920s, covered bridges were on the way out. The modern state highway system developed in the same decade and destroyed all sorts of old bridges left and right.

The new highways brought tourists, who began to view covered bridges in a new light. Just as the bridges began disappearing rapidly, they became special relics of an endangered past. Rosalie Wells' classic *Covered Bridges in America* was the first book on the subject from an antiquarian point of view. Henry Ford imported a covered bridge from Pennsylvania in 1937 for his Greenfield Village museum near Detroit, which was a celebration of the older countryside. By the late 1960s, covered bridges became recognized historic treasures, but only after many decades of huge losses from what was known as "the inevitable march of progress."

Origins: Why Were Bridges Covered?

Europe has had covered bridges since the late Middle Ages. They may have originated in Switzerland, where timber is abundant. Wood seems like a temporary building material; if exposed to the weather, it rots. When it is protected indoors, however, it lasts indefinitely. The Swiss covered their wooden bridges to make them last longer, and several examples in service today are centuries old.

The covered bridge can be a truss bridge, a combination of truss and arch, or in rare cases, simply an arch. The huge beams inside make a framework to allow the bridge to span an open space, while being supported only at the ends. Timber truss or arch bridges can also be built without roofing and side boarding, and they still have the same framework of beams. They do not last very long that way, and their visual appeal is different, but these non-covered bridges are nearly the same as covered ones from an engineering point of view.

Roofed bridges of an entirely different kind have been around for centuries in Asia and southern Europe, namely China, Vietnam, and Italy. Their bridges are not of truss construction and seem to have been covered to protect the traveler rather than the structure. In the traditional covered bridge of America and northern Europe, the covering protects the trussed framework of the bridge itself from decay.

The idea of a covered bridge took centuries to cross the Atlantic. Great Britain never had covered bridges except for one nineteenth century example, which was built in romantic imitation of Switzerland's bridges. There were a few open wooden bridges, but stone was the favored material. As for France and the Low Countries, covered bridges were also unknown. Most of the early European settlers of eastern North America were unfamiliar with the concept. The covered truss bridge was reinvented in America where timber was plentiful, but stone was either rare or expensive to cut and to transport.

This is Cooley Bridge over Furnace Brook in Pittsford, Vermont, as it looked in the 1920s when automobile touring was beginning to take off. *Basil Kievit, Richard Sanders Allen Collection, NSPCB Archives*

Side boards have been missing from this covered bridge for years, and important structural timbers are beginning to decay. The wood is still sound only a few inches away where it has been protected from the weather.

The last covered bridge in Alaska served a gold mine north of Hyder, in the southern part of the panhandle near the British Columbia border. It was destroyed by an avalanche in 1978, and this view shows damage from an earlier snowslide on the left end. Alaska had seven known covered bridges, but now they are all gone.

America's first known plan for a covered bridge was published in an anonymous article in the January 1787 *Columbian Magazine*. There was no explanation for the roof and side boarding, so the idea seemed to already have been familiar. This is a mystery because there are no records of any covered bridges being built that early. The first documented American covered bridge spanned the Schuylkill River just west of Philadelphia, and was completed in 1805. The plan in the article resembled one later patented by Theodore Burr, but Burr was only 15 years old at the time and is unlikely to have written the article.

10

Shortly after the article was published, the covered bridge idea appeared in Canada, a country that long maintained intellectual contact with continental Europe. The reputation of Swiss builder Hans Ulrich Grubenmann spread widely in educated circles after the construction of his long-span covered bridge in Schaffhausen in 1755–57. A bridge inspired by Grubenmann was proposed for the east end of Montreal Island around 1805, but the exact details of the plan are unknown.

When covered bridge construction began in America shortly after 1800, it was an idea with perfect timing. Within three decades, the covered bridge became the standard for important river crossings.

This covered bridge crosses Meech Brook in the Gatineau Valley near Farm Point, Quebec, not far from Canada's capital in Ottawa, Ontario. The Quebec government built hundreds of covered bridges in the first half of the twentieth century, and they were sometimes known simply as *ponts rouges* (red bridges) because of the color they were originally painted.

The Melcher Bridge in Parke County, Indiana, is typical of the hundreds of Burr trusses that once served roads in the eastern and central United States.

COVERED BRIDGES FOR TOLL TURNPIKES
1805-1860

Philadelphia was America's leading city in 1800, but it was hemmed in on a peninsula between the Schuylkill and Delaware rivers. To the west, development lay beckoning, and the city needed to be connected with this region by a long-lasting bridge.

The Schuylkill River's "Permanent Bridge" was America's first known covered bridge and was built in 1800–05. As originally planned by Massachusetts bridge builder Timothy Palmer, it did not have a covering. At the request of Judge Richard Peters, who was a bridge company stockholder, Palmer changed his plans to include a roof and siding to protect the bridge from the elements. He said, "There are some that say I argue much against my own interest" in becoming an advocate of covered bridges since he would have more work if bridges decayed sooner. According to Thomas Pope, an early historian of bridges, "He considered the Schuylkill Bridge superstructure the most perfect of any he has built."

Unforeseen transportation changes required the replacement of this Permanent Bridge in 1850 with a new structure that could carry railroads. No trace of it remains, although the site is easy to find. It is where Market Street crosses the Schuylkill River just east of Amtrak's 30th Street Station in Philadelphia. Palmer's structure set the pattern for the earliest covered bridges; it had two separate lanes for travel, and its covering had a decorative finish.

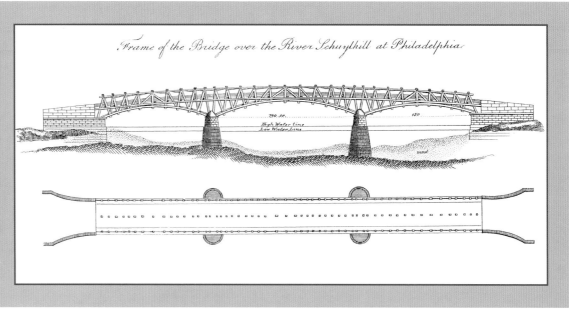

Frame of the Bridge over the River Schuylkill at Philadelphia

Grand Early Turnpike Bridges, 1805-1820

Sculptor William Rush, who specialized in figureheads for ships, decorated the Schuylkill Permanent Bridge with allegorical statues of commerce and agriculture. The lower part of the bridge's side boards was finished in paint sprinkled with stone dust to look like masonry. All the early covered bridges were highly ornamented and wide enough for two lanes of travel, and most had sidewalks.

Covered bridges were expensive to construct, so at first they served only those locations that could well afford them or wherever the volume of traffic was high enough to repay investors in a reasonable time. Before 1820, private capital was the motive force in transportation improvements. The government was not involved in highways except for the National Road. Joint-stock toll companies built bridges and roads, and their managers were proud of their creations. This is why such care went into the coverings. Cynics might later grumble that a grander bridge would require a higher toll, but whatever the reason, the structures were beautiful.

Once a covered bridge was created in one of America's greatest cities, they became the rage. They appeared on the Delaware River in Trenton, New Jersey, and in Easton, Pennsylvania, by 1806. Soon New York state, New England, and the South had covered bridges. In Newburyport, Massachusetts, the 1792 Deer Island Bridge received a cover around 1810, which confuses historians. The bridge was older than the first covered bridge at Philadelphia, but did not get its roof until later.

None of the grand early turnpike bridges survive today. They served the busiest travel arteries and were so important they were made permanent by being covered.

14

Their locations likewise meant they were the first to be doomed by increased traffic. Many early bridges had arched floors and clearances too low to be adapted for railroads, a use the early builders could not have foreseen. They received much attention in their day because of their novelty, and at least they are well documented.

Mr. Palmer, Mr. Burr, and Mr. Wernwag

These first covered bridges were all custom structures. Certain builders were known for a particular style, but they designed each job to meet the occasion. Later, architects patented standard plans that other builders adapted for use. In the period of early turnpike bridges, the architect and the bridge builder were often the same person, and engineering was not yet a separate profession.

The giant among the bridge builders at the turn of the nineteenth century was Timothy Palmer of Newburyport, Massachusetts. His Schuylkill Permanent Bridge was built near the end of his career. He was born in 1751 and he did not begin building until the age of 40. He was busy throughout the 1790s and bridged New England rivers such as the Merrimack, Connecticut, and the Kennebec with big, non-covered bridges.

Palmer's style was a trussed arch. It is an overall arched framework assembled of many smaller pieces. The bridge floor followed the bottom of the arch up and down. In later bridges, Palmer framed the floor partway up the sides to minimize the hump. He patented his plan in 1797. Other builders used his technique, but it appears Palmer was involved in some way with all these projects as a designer.

Theodore Burr, Palmer's contemporary, has a quite different story. He was born in 1771 in Torringford, Connecticut. Some early historians described him as a relative of Aaron Burr, but he was not. Burr began his career in Oxford, New York, and went on to bridge major rivers such as the Mohawk and the upper Hudson. At first he tried various plans, usually with success, although one ill-fated suspension bridge experiment at Schenectady had to be propped up later with extra piers. The plan he finally settled upon was highly durable and is known as the Burr truss, which was patented in 1806 and 1817.

Burr's design was also a trussed arch, but he superimposed a separate arch onto a truss frame with a level floor. This advantage was obvious in lengthy bridges of more than one span, and it later proved adaptable for railroads. Burr's plan was not really new, because it had already appeared in print in the 1787 *Columbian Magazine* article. Details of the patent are not well known because a fire at the Patent Office destroyed the early records. It is possible that Burr may have intended to patent an advanced construction method for a general plan he found already in use, but he was the first to build bridges widely according to the truss plan that still bears his name. He began his career slightly later than Palmer, and most of his bridges were covered from the start.

Among Theodore Burr's many achievements was the construction of the longest single-span wooden truss across the narrows of the Susquehanna River in McCall's Ferry, Pennsylvania. The main span was a whopping 360 feet between the piers. Burr had to

Timothy Palmer, with Moody Spofford, bridged the Merrimack River in Haverhill, Massachusetts, in 1794, but the first bridge was not covered. It gave way in 1808 to a second bridge on Palmer's trussed arch design (shown here), which was afterwards covered, and lasted until about 1875. *Richard Sanders Allen Collection, NSPCB Archives*

There are no Palmer trusses still in existence, but there are two bridges with trussed arch frames that remotely show his influence. One is the Humpback Bridge near Covington, Virginia, which was built in 1857. The other example is in southern Ohio.

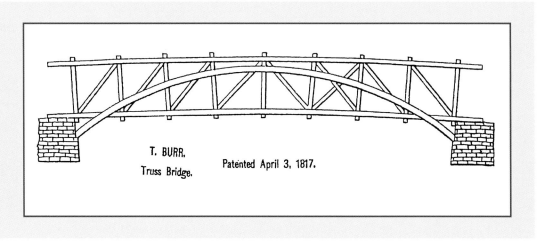

T. BURR.
Truss Bridge.
Paténted April 3, 1817.

use floats and river ice for support to build the bridge during the winter of 1814–15 because the channel was too deep and the current was too swift to set up falsework in the river. An immense ice jam tore the bridge out three years later. Burr had been paid with toll company stock and took a tremendous loss. A replacement bridge was never built.

The Burr truss was widely used by others in later periods of bridge building. Unfortunately the man himself benefited little from this development. He was a first rate builder, but a poor businessman. Despite a productive career, he died in poverty in 1822.

A third builder of elaborate early turnpike bridges was German-born Lewis Wernwag. He was active in the Philadelphia area and completed major covered bridges on the Schuylkill in Upper Ferry (Fairmount) in 1812, and on the Delaware in New Hope in 1814. The former structure was proudly named "The Colossus" and had a single span of 340 feet. Before the temporary falsework was about to be knocked away during the opening day ceremonies, the bridge company directors feared their project might fall into the river. Wernwag calmly invited them to check the construction blocks on which the bridge rested. They were all loose. Wernwag had set the bridge firmly on its abutments the day before and it was already supporting itself.

Wernwag used various combinations of arch and truss and took out several patents. Although he influenced later builders, his plans were only occasionally used by others. In later years, he favored a truss with a level floor similar to the Burr plan, but with radically flared posts. This "Wernwag truss" had an added arch built up of several ribs he often placed inside a doubled set of trusses. The usual form of the Burr truss was also a sandwich, but the arches were on the outsides of a single plane of trusswork.

Later Turnpike Bridges, 1820-1860

By 1820 the covered bridge was no longer a novelty. It was a standard structure wherever it could be afforded. By now the usefulness of a covering was obvious. No

16

one yet knew how long a covered bridge might last, but since non-covered bridges were usually good for only 15 years or so, the extra expense for a roof and side boarding was a wise investment.

As covered bridges became standard, they also became less ornate. Some continued to be built by private toll companies until the Civil War or even afterwards, but the later corporate directors saw less need to be flamboyant. Their bridges often still had two lanes for travel, but the carvings and fancy windows of the first generation of covered bridges were gone. The later turnpike bridges were often spartan with no decoration at all. They now appeared in small towns and rural places, but were still on important travel routes.

Enslow Bridge in Perry County, Pennsylvania, shows the elegant simplicity of Theodore Burr's truss as it was commonly built. Note that a separate arch is bolted to a truss frame instead of forming the entire bridge into an arch as Palmer had done.

For longer spans, the Burr truss sometimes used two concentric arches. This covered bridge over the Delaware River between Columbia, New Jersey, and Portland, Pennsylvania, was destroyed by a flood in 1955. *Raymond Brainerd, NSPCB Archives*

The covered bridges of the National Road were part of the later turnpike era, but the road was an anomaly. In a time when private capital built major travel routes, the National Road was a federal government project. It was not a toll road and it eventually ran from Cumberland, Maryland, to Vandalia, Illinois. The larger rivers usually had two-lane covered bridges, but they are all long gone, although several stone arch bridges still exist.

A few plain-styled covered bridges from the late turnpike era survive in places where the traffic patterns have since changed. The only feature which distinguishes them from bridges of a later era that were built by towns or counties for purely local use is the fact that they commonly have two lanes for travel, separated by a third set of trusses that divide the bridge down the middle. These structures are known as double-barrel bridges.

Cheat River Bridge near Erwin, West Virginia, was the last existing covered bridge designed by Lewis Wernwag. It was destroyed by fire in 1964. *Oscar Lane Collection, NSPCB Archives*

The later turnpike bridges were usually not the products of virtuoso architects, who both designed and built innovative structures from the ground up. By now, a few patent plans of proven durability had become established. Local builders followed or adapted them and paid fees for their use as long as the patents were in force. This pattern is also characteristic of the classic era of single-lane, publicly built covered bridges, which overlapped the late turnpike period in time.

Theodore Burr used several experimental plans before he settled on the truss that bears his name. He used laminated arches for this bridge over the Delaware River between Trenton, New Jersey, and Morrisville, Pennsylvania, which was opened in 1806. This photograph shows it being demolished after the covering had been removed.

The double-barrel bridge over Tygart's Valley River in Philippi, West Virginia, was a toll bridge built for a turnpike in 1852. Today it serves U.S. Route 250, and is the last covered bridge in service on a U.S. numbered highway. This is how it looked in 1975 before it was heavily damaged by fire and rebuilt.

The original version of Pulp Mill Bridge between Middlebury and Weybridge, Vermont, was built for a toll turnpike company. This is a replacement built by public funds in the 1850s, but it is in the style of the old turnpike bridges.

2

Krepps Bridge in Washington County, Pennsylvania, is a kingpost truss with additional timbers underneath the main braces, known as subpanel bracing.

COVERED BRIDGES OF THE CLASSIC ERA 1830-1920

Most existing covered bridges are not relics of forgotten turnpikes and were never toll bridges. Shortly before 1830, town and county governments began to specify covered bridges for construction on their local roads. Single-lane structures usually satisfied such needs, and there was rarely expense for ornament beyond the very simplest kind. In the Northeast, town governments usually contracted for the bridges. From Pennsylvania on westward, counties were more often responsible.

These are the classic covered bridges of the popular imagination. It would be impossible to say how many were built, but surely more than 10,000. Construction lasted about a century. New England and the Middle Atlantic states stopped building them soon after 1900, but they held on in parts of the Midwest until around 1920, and occasionally in the South into the 1930s. Canada and the American West built covered bridges through the mid-1950s, but these will be described in a later chapter because they were built under circumstances different from those of the classic era.

Local builders used a wide variety of patent designs, whose differences are obvious after a peek inside. Theodore Burr's arch-truss combination was a holdover from the early turnpike era, and it was widely used throughout Pennsylvania, the upper South, much of the Midwest, and parts of New England. Inventors devised new plans to meet the growing demand for bridges in a rapidly expanding nation where labor was often scarce. They also tried ingenious ways to address or avoid various problems of using wood for a structural material: joints subjected to tension are difficult to construct efficiently and wood needs to be seasoned. To understand what the inventors were doing, one must know how a truss bridge functions.

The Structure of a Truss Bridge

If a bridge is needed where there is timber long enough to span the gap in one piece, no truss is required at all. A few long beams will do the job. This primitive style was used until very recently in lumbering regions where large timber was readily available. Since World War II, immense beams of steel, reinforced concrete, and glue-laminated timber have been used to build bridges. Although much work and knowledge is involved to make these materials, when in place, they are like an ancient log bridge; long beams under the floor do all the work.

Coburn Bridge in East Montpelier, Vermont, is a covered bridge from the classic era. The photograph is a perfect example of the old New England roadside.

Where longer spans were needed and the available timber was too short, it had to be joined together in a framework of some kind. One possibility is an arch, but an arch of timber segments cannot stand alone. It needs extra bracing because uneven loading would pull it apart. The Swiss designed many wooden bridges using a pure arch boxed inside square panels for support, but this style wasn't common in America. Instead, Americans joined an arch with a truss framework, as Theodore Burr and his contemporaries did in various ways. Later designers preferred a truss structure with no arch.

A truss is a rigid frame built from combinations of triangles, which carries the load to the ends of the bridge by alternately pulling and pushing the individual parts. Members that are pulled are in tension, and those that are pushed are in compression. In some truss designs, each member has only one function. In others, the same member can serve in tension or in compression, depending on where the load is located.

Pool Forge Bridge is a classic covered bridge from Lancaster County, Pennsylvania. For many years, nearly all the county's covered bridges had white portals and red sides. In recent years they have been redone in a variety of styles.

Sim Smith Bridge in Parke County, Indiana, is a classic era covered bridge from the Midwest.

The simplest trusses date to medieval times and were used for roof framing and bridges. The kingpost truss has a single center post. The kingpost, with a diagonal brace on either side of it, carries the load down to the ends of the truss, where it rests on the abutments. The center of the bridge floor hangs from the kingpost, which is in tension, while the braces are in compression. At the ends of the bridge, the downward force of the load is supported on the abutments, but since the braces are diagonal, there is outward thrust. This is transmitted to the bottom horizontal member or "chord," which ties the truss together and prevents the braces from spreading. Like the kingpost, the chord is in tension.

The queenpost truss, which has been used for many years, is slightly more complicated. Instead of a single kingpost, there are two vertical queenposts spaced some distance apart. This truss functions like the other, but its floor is hung from two places so it can support longer spans. There is a top chord in compression between the tops of the queenposts.

26

For longer bridges, there is the multiple kingpost truss, which is another inheritance from medieval times. A long frame supports a series of vertical posts, and a brace between each post inclines towards the center of the bridge. The posts and the bottom chord are all in tension; the braces and top chord are in compression. One can visualize the load being transmitted by a series of pulls on the posts and pushes on the braces, in zigzag fashion, all the way to the ends of the bridge. This truss, when combined with an arch, is known as the Burr truss. In a few areas, the multiple kingpost truss is loosely called a Burr truss even without the arch.

All of these trusses have been used for covered bridges in Europe and the United States. There is a certain waste involved in using wood for members that are in tension. They must be notched together so they won't slide apart. The piece is only as strong as its thinnest part, where it is notched. The extra thickness elsewhere is unneeded wood. Even where big timber was plentiful, this was a problem because it increased the weight of the bridge. The biggest load a timber bridge must carry is its own weight, known to engineers as the dead load.

Tension joints are expensive to construct because they require much labor. Timbers that are always in compression do not have these problems, though. They are held in place by the force pressing on them from both ends. All of their thickness is used since they do not need to be notched. The first answer to these design challenges appeared on the scene in 1820.

Ithiel Town and the Lattice Truss

Ithiel Town, an architect, was born in Thompson, Connecticut, in 1784. He is remembered today for his important role in developing the Greek Revival style of architecture, along with his partner Alexander Jackson Davis. Town undertook major projects, churches and other public edifices, including state capitol buildings, and some still stand today. He also designed one of the most widely used wooden bridge trusses that he patented in 1820 and 1835.

The Town truss was a lattice of sawn planks that didn't use large dimension timber or iron. It is sometimes called the lattice truss or the Town lattice truss, and it inspired a few other designs of the same general type, which weren't as popular. Large wooden pegs called treenails held the joints; the word is pronounced "trunnels" and sometimes spelled that way. Other wooden trusses used a few treenails to pin the joints, but they were smaller and less numerous than in the Town plan. The treenail joints did not require notching. There was some labor involved in boring holes, but a large section of plank carried the load for a minimum of wasted material.

The Town truss is one where the members of its web can serve in tension or compression. In this plan, the load is spread over a wide network. As in all trusses, the top chord is normally in compression and the bottom chord is in tension. In bridges of more than one span, however, a Town truss could be built as one long continuous framework over the intermediate piers instead of having separate truss structures butted end for end.

This simple log bridge was photographed in 1977 on Route 37 north of Kitwanga, British Columbia. Logs underneath support the floor, and logs alongside the deck serve as primitive guardrails.

This bridge at Brunnen, Switzerland, is typical of the complicated trusswork found in central Europe. It has an arch frame boxed inside square panels and queenpost bracing.

27

Many kingpost bridges were never covered. This former example near Parkindale, New Brunswick, had shingles over the braces to give some protection from the weather. It had a steel rod instead of a wooden kingpost and added outrigger buttresses to prevent sway.

Multi-span bridges are stronger if they can be built continuously, but they can experience stress reversal during certain loadings. The joints in Town trusses can handle these stresses.

One minor drawback to the Town plan was that it required more space on the abutments or piers at the ends of the spans. Other trusses concentrated the load on a small point at either end of the bridge, but a Town truss spread it out over a length of several feet that had to be supported on a long corbelled foot, usually with big abutments. Stonework was always expensive, but on the other hand, Burr trusses also required massive masonry to offset the thrust at the arch ends. Later bridge patent designs allowed for smaller abutments. In some areas, Town truss builders met the challenge and modified the ends of the lattice with fanlike bracing to concentrate the load on a smaller area, or by using freestanding piers placed a short way in from the end of the truss with cantilevered foot timbers to distribute the load.

Town lattice trusses are still found throughout New England and New York. In Pennsylvania, the Town truss occasionally caught the fancy of county commissioners, although the commonwealth is usually noted for Burr trusses. The Town lattice design was popular everywhere south of Virginia because the architect had extensive business connections in North Carolina and built a couple of influential prototype bridges in the area. A variant of the Town plan was used in Quebec's covered bridges up through the 1950s, so the truss was actively used for over a century.

Ithiel Town was so busy with other projects that he built few bridges himself. Those he did build served high-traffic locations where they have long since been replaced. Town collected patent royalties, said to be a dollar per linear foot of bridge, or two dollars if a builder was caught using the plan without paying first. Lattice trusses thought to be by Town himself still hold up the roof of the First Presbyterian Church in Fayetteville, North Carolina. The architect was working there when he filed his first bridge patent in 1820. The existing roof trusses date from around 1832, when he was called back to help rebuild Fayetteville after a disastrous downtown fire.

This queenpost truss has extra subpanel bracing to span a longer distance. Flint Bridge in Tunbridge, Vermont, was built in 1874 by Ira Mudgett.

Flint Bridge measures 87 feet, which is about the maximum a queenpost truss can span. It crosses First Branch White River.

Above: **The former covered bridge near Logan Mills in Clinton County, Pennsylvania, was another queenpost truss.**

The Long Truss

Colonel Stephen H. Long was born in Hopkinton, New Hampshire, in 1784. Long is still remembered today for his frontier exploration as a topographical engineer with the U.S. Army, but he patented a bridge truss of his own in 1830, which enjoyed a vogue for over 20 years.

The Long truss is a frame of paired upright posts. In the panel between each set of posts is a pair of diagonal braces that incline towards the center of the bridge. It is like a

Left: **Blaisdell Bridge, near East Randolph, Vermont, has only half-height trusswork, but otherwise it is a typical example of the multiple kingpost truss.**

32

The multiple kingpost truss was widely used in southeastern Ohio. This is the former Jesse Johnson Bridge over Opossum Run near Mount Ephraim in Noble County.

Parrish Bridge, over Olive Green Creek, south of Sharon in Noble County, Ohio, shows the capable span length of the multiple kingpost truss. The bridge still exists, but it has been bypassed since this photograph was taken in 1976.

double-thickness multiple kingpost truss, but each panel has a single counterbrace that goes the other way. It looks like a series of Xs in wooden boxes, but so do some later covered bridge plans that are often misidentified as Long trusses. The patented Long bridge is rare today. It always has two braces and one counterbrace per panel—all in compression—with paired vertical posts in tension. It was a very sturdy bridge, but required much custom framing and fell out of favor when the colonel stopped promoting it.

The Long truss is of interest to engineers because it involves the modern principle of prestressing. Wooden trusses can be extremely strong, but wood is surprisingly elastic and most wooden bridges flex noticeably under load. This does not make them unsafe, but it does make an analysis of the stresses difficult. As the truss is compressed, the joints shift position slightly and the loads are transmitted differently from the way they are when the truss is not under load. The stresses also change with loads traveling at different speeds. If a truss can be constructed so that it behaves as if permanently loaded, a more precise analysis of the joints is possible because they always bear the same way. A more rigid bridge was of special interest to railroads.

The counterbraces of a Long truss perform this function. When properly stressed by wedges, they resist the action of the unloaded bridge to spring back up. The load is transmitted the same way all the time assuming the bridge is properly maintained. In

Kingsley Bridge, near East Clarendon, Vermont, was a typical example of the Town lattice truss. It still exists, but much of the original trusswork has been replaced since this view, circa 1974.

Sunday River Bridge in Newry, Maine, shows several kinds of elaborate notching used for tension joints in timber construction.

Kingsley Bridge stands high over Vermont's rock-strewn Mill River, and is not far from Rutland State Airport.

the early twentieth century, engineers slighted the Long truss because the counter-braces made the truss redundant. It was hard to tell exactly how much load was being carried by the braces and counterbraces unless the bridge was overloaded and the counterbraces stopped working. Computers now allow these stresses to be modeled with greater precision, and engineers have come to appreciate the Long truss for introducing prestressing.

The Long truss is historically important because it probably formed the basis for an invention by William Howe that revolutionized and vastly extended the period of wooden bridge construction.

The Howe Truss

William Howe was born in 1803 in Spencer, Massachusetts. He built mills and churches before he turned his attention to bridges. His nephew Elias invented the sewing machine. William Howe's special concern was for bridge trusses that could be easily adjusted. The Long truss could be adjusted, but only to a small extent because the wedges were of limited size. If more adjustment was possible, then a bridge could be built quickly with unseasoned lumber, and later fine-tuned as the timber began to shrink. Such a feature would be a big advantage in the rapidly expanding United States of the 1840s where railroads created a huge demand for new bridges in a hurry.

Howe devised several adjustable plans, but his early designs were elaborate and cumbersome to frame. His first plan, patented in 1840, had a double, overlapping web of braces with wooden posts split and spread with wedges for adjustment, but no such bridges are known to have been built. The second plan, also patented in 1840, kept the double web of braces, but replaced the posts with adjustable iron rods. This vaguely resembled a lattice truss, although it operated quite differently because the braces served only in compression. A few of these double-web Howe trusses were built in the U.S., but they are all long gone. The plan still survives in Europe. George Washington Whistler, a business partner of Howe's, brought the truss to Russia in the 1840s, and the design showed up on railroads in Norway two decades later, long after Whistler died. A few double-web Howe trusses still serve roads in central Europe, and one of them crosses the Rhine from Switzerland to Liechtenstein's capital of Vaduz.

Meanwhile back home, Howe simplified his invention to a set of boxed Xs that, in profile, looked like a Long truss with two braces and one counterbrace per panel, all in compression. Howe used iron rods instead of vertical wooden posts. The rods allowed greater adjustment than what was possible with an all-wood truss. He didn't patent this apparent knock-off, but his 1846 design came close and he had trouble with Colonel Long.

This final simpler plan is known as the Howe truss in the U.S. today, and it was wildly successful. Its ready adjustability was a completely new feature, and it was much easier to frame than the older trusses. It could be built with unseasoned lumber and it solved the problem of wasted wood in tension joints by replacing them with iron, held in place by bolts. The lower chord was wood because although it was also in tension, it usually doubled as a support for the floor system.

This detail of the long-gone Dean Bridge over Otter Creek in Brandon, Vermont, shows how the Town lattice truss is held together with treenails.

Bath-Haverhill Bridge, over the Ammonoosuc River in Woodsville, New Hampshire, was bypassed in 1999 after 170 years of service. It is America's oldest existing Town lattice truss.

Above: This is a closeup of the ends of the Town lattice trusswork in New Hampshire's Bath-Haverhill Bridge, which was built in 1829. In the background you can see some steel cable bracing added to stabilize the bridge temporarily while it awaits restoration.

Above, right: A peek underneath Bath-Haverhill Bridge shows a remarkably interesting floor system. Historians believe that one set of floor beams may be original, but the system was modified when laminated arches were later added.

Bridge building had come a long way with the invention of the Howe truss. Sometimes local builders used the plan as they had with the older patents, but now precut parts could be shipped by rail to the site and speedily erected. This may seem contrary to our understanding of old-time craftsmanship, but the Howe truss became one of the most widely used plans for covered bridges throughout the country. It co-existed with the older Burr and Town trusses that retained strong regional popularity into the twentieth century.

A few other early truss inventions were used here and there, but none were as popular as the Burr, Town, and Howe. These were the truss plans that bridged America during the classic era of covered bridges, but what about the contractors who built them?

Bridge Builders and Part-Time Farmers

Most covered bridges of the classic era were the products of men who specialized in this work, although they often worked in other areas, such as farming or mill construction. One of the best known in New England was Nichols Montgomery Powers of Clarendon, Vermont. His first name somehow came down to posterity as Nicholas, but either way, Nick Powers was born in 1817 in the hills behind Proctor, Vermont, and took up bridge building at the tender age of 20. His first project spanned Furnace Brook in Pittsford Mills, but because he was still a minor, his father had to sign the contract for him and promise to make good for any ruined timbers. The bridge served for close to a hundred years, and was only removed because it had become too narrow for the traffic when

This view, taken in 2002, shows Bath-Haverhill Bridge in need of restoration. Work is scheduled to begin soon.

U.S. Route 7 took over the road it served. During construction of its replacement, a 20-ton steamroller used the covered bridge.

Powers favored the Town lattice truss and built many bridges in Vermont. In the 1850s and 1860s he went further afield and built an immense double-barrel Long truss in North Blenheim, New York, in 1855. The central truss incorporates an arch, and reaches to the tall roof ridge. Blenheim Bridge looks very heavy, and as it neared completion the local wisdom was that it would tumble into Schoharie Creek as soon as the falsework was removed. Powers declared that if the bridge went down, he would go with it. The bridge still stands today. Documentation from the 1930s shows that it originally measured 210 feet between the abutments under the central truss, although it has been modified by recent repairs.

The Town lattice truss was popular in New England and the South. This lengthy and beautiful example is in Blount County, Alabama. Even the upper lateral bracing is in lattice form.

In 1866, Powers joined a crew that was building a very long multispan railroad bridge over the mouth of the Susquehanna River at Havre de Grace, Maryland. Amtrak crosses at about the same place today. He signed on as a boss carpenter, but was later promoted to superintendent of construction after a windstorm partially destroyed the unfinished bridge and the original superintendent was fired. An old story says that he drew plans on the side of a block of timber and completed them in just a few hours time. The job kept Powers in Maryland for a long time, and his wife wrote from Vermont and asked him to come home. He promised to return the moment the bridge was done, and did so. He missed the opening day celebration with the crossing of the first train, and he never traveled so far from home again.

Many Powers-built bridges still stand. His last one, the Brown Bridge over Cold River in Shrewsbury, Vermont, dates from 1880. It is a tried and true Town lattice, just like his first bridge in Pittsford Mills some 43 years earlier.

Nichols M. Powers was a professional bridge builder, but he also worked in the marble industry, did rigging and railroad work, and had a farm and a cheese factory. He was not college educated, but had a good practical knowledge of engineering and could perform complex mathematical calculations in his head.

James F. Tasker of Cornish, New Hampshire, was a part-time bridge builder. During the warm season he was a farmer, but after the harvest's tasks were over, he built bridges from lumber cut on his own woodlot. Tasker was an interesting fellow who won contracts by visiting country fairs with a small bridge model. He would drive his horse over the model as a demonstration of strength. A number of his bridges still serve traffic today.

Although Pennsylvania is better known for Burr trusses, a few counties, including Bucks County, opted for the Town lattice plan. This is the view from under the bridge at Uhlerstown, which is America's only covered bridge that spans a canal.

Peter Paddleford of Littleton, New Hampshire, was also a famous New England builder. He used the Long truss for his first covered bridges, but then devised his own plan. The Paddleford truss was never patented, but it developed an important regional following and was still being built four decades after the inventor's death in 1859. Several other major New England builders such as Charles and Frank Broughton of Conway, New Hampshire, made the Paddleford design their truss of choice. It is found today from the Western Mountains of Maine, across northern New Hampshire, and into the Northeast Kingdom of Vermont.

Meanwhile in Canada, Montreal's location on an island offered many opportunities for bridge builders. The St. Lawrence River in front of the city never had a wooden bridge, but Pascal Persillier Lachapelle spanned the river des Prairies to the north with several long, impressive wooden structures. Peter Paddleford was called in from New

The covered bridge over Fitch Bay Narrows at Lake Memphremagog in Quebec is a Town lattice truss, and demonstrates the international appeal of this plan. The bridge still stands, but was bypassed shortly after this photograph was taken in 1975.

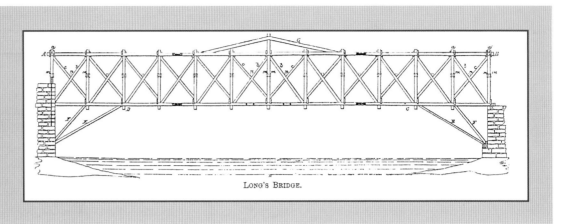

The Long truss is shown here as it looked in Colonel Stephen H. Long's 1830 patent. In practice, the extra struts under the bridge and the kingpost-like frame on top were soon eliminated.

LONG'S BRIDGE.

Hampshire to give an estimate for a bridge off the east end of the island over to Repentigny, but the job fell through because finances were unavailable.

In New York State, Scottish-born Robert Murray built notable Long trusses in the western regions of the Catskills. From his home in the lovely hill town of Andes, Murray is said to have walked the many miles to his job sites every Monday morning, and back home on Saturdays, carrying his shoes to avoid wearing them out.

Pennsylvania today has more covered bridges than any other state, but their builders are little known for the most part. In many cases, even their names are forgotten, especially in the western part of the commonwealth. In the southeast, Elias McMellen built immaculately framed Burr trusses on massive masonry abutments, flanked by long stone parapet approaches. This was a regional style used by many lesser known builders as well.

One of the South's best known builders was Horace King of Georgia. Born a slave in 1807, he served a noted builder, John Godwin, and his talent as a framer helped his

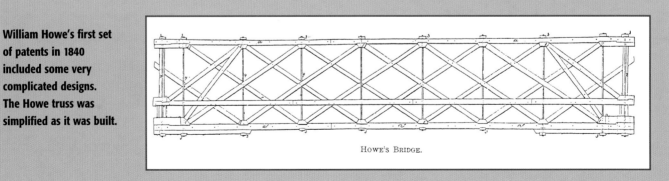

William Howe's first set of patents in 1840 included some very complicated designs. The Howe truss was simplified as it was built.

HOWE'S BRIDGE.

44

master win many contracts. Godwin freed King in 1846 so King could pursue a career on his own. The two remained friends, and when Godwin died, Horace King placed a special memorial tablet on his grave at Phenix City, Alabama.

The Civil War wreaked heavy destruction on the covered bridges of the South, for they were easy targets by fire, and many were later rebuilt by Horace King. His career spanned 40 years, and his sons and a grandson became bridge builders as well.

Ohio has long been a stronghold of covered bridges and is second only to Pennsylvania in numbers today. Their builders worked mostly locally and sometimes built a dozen or more spans, often all in the same county. One of the best remembered was Blue Jeans Brandt of Lancaster, Ohio, who framed bridges in his immense front yard, then brought the precut pieces on site for quick assembly. August Borneman of the Hocking Valley Bridge Works was another noted Ohio builder.

Indiana had a famous three-generation bridgebuilding family, the Kennedys of Rushville. Archibald M. Kennedy started the business in 1870, assisted by his son Emmett as building superintendent, and son Charles was in charge of supply. The senior Kennedy negotiated the contracts and served as salesman. He had a small model he would stand on to demonstrate its strength—and he was a large man. Archibald later retired and Charles turned to other business, but Emmett carried on with his two sons until 1918.

The former Wolf Bridge over Spoon River in Knox County, Illinois, was how the Howe truss was usually built. It was destroyed by arson and later rebuilt in a similar style.

Howe trusses are common in covered bridges of the Midwest. This is the North Pole Bridge in Brown County, Ohio, as it looked in 1974.

The former Squilax Bridge over Shuswap Lake near Chase, British Columbia, was never covered, but it is an excellent example of the Howe truss. It also had a short draw span near one end.

Kennedy-built covered bridges are among the most easily recognized because unlike most structures of the classic era, they are highly ornamented. The white-painted portal is shaped in a graceful arch decorated with scrollwork at the sides, and finely turned brackets grace the gable overhang. Rushville, Circleville, East Connersville, and Shelbyville once had Kennedy bridges with gallery-like sidewalks on either side, and two of them had boarded arched ceilings inside. These grand village bridges are gone, but several more modest country spans remain. Their last few bridges were built during World War I and lacked the scrollwork and brackets, but the graceful arched entry remained as a Kennedy signature.

Parke County in western Indiana still has 30 covered bridges, which is more than any other county in the United States. It was also home to two very famous bridge

builders. Joseph J. Daniels originally worked in Ohio, where his father had been an agent for Stephen H. Long. He gradually moved west and settled in Parke's county seat of Rockville in 1861. He built bridges large and small in Parke and adjacent counties until 1904. Daniels' competitor Joseph A. Britton was born in a log cabin near Rockville, and built dozens of covered bridges right up to 1920. Both men and the Kennedys usually used the Burr truss, but each builder evolved his own style of framing the joints and building the housing.

In Madison County, Iowa, builder H. P. Jones used the Town lattice truss with two unusual details. He balanced them on narrow steel caisson piers, and his bridges have nearly flat roofs.

The West Coast also had covered bridges in the classic era. In Oregon, A. S. Miller & Sons, and Lord Nelson Roney were the two most prolific builders. Many of their bridges were replaced with more modern covered bridges during the course of the twentieth century. Scholars can detect influence from the earlier builders' housing styles in the later structures.

Nichols Powers' first covered bridge, which was built in 1837 when he was 20 years old, was removed in 1931. It was on what is now U.S. Route 7 in Pittsford Mills, Vermont. This view looks down what is now State Route 3 towards the road junction and the bridge.

Nichols Powers' double-barrel masterpiece over Schoharie Creek in North Blenheim, New York, has the longest clear span, measuring from truss seat to truss seat, of any existing covered bridge in America, as it was originally built. However, the 210-foot distance between the abutment faces is tied with a covered bridge in Nevada County, California.

Sunday River Bridge in Newry, Maine, is a well-built example of the truss style developed by Peter Paddleford of Littleton, New Hampshire. Note the elongated ties that help spread the load over a larger area of the truss.

Sunday River Bridge was bypassed in 1958, but it is kept in excellent condition by the Maine Department of Transportation.

Bennett Bridge in Wilsons Mills, Maine, is another Paddleford truss. This view was taken in 1973. The bridge is now closed.

Beaverkill Campsite Bridge in Sullivan County, New York, was built around 1865 by John Davidson, a lumberman from the Catskills.

Dreibelbis Bridge crosses Maiden Creek near Lenhartsville in Berks County, Pennsylvania, and dates from 1869. False front portals of various styles were once found on many southeastern Pennsylvania covered bridges, but are very rare today.

South Bridge in Perry County, Ohio, is shown dressed up with special paint for the national bicentennial, but otherwise it was a typical southeastern Ohio covered bridge. The trusswork still exists, but the bridge has been greatly modernized since this photograph was taken.

Rex's Bridge in Lehigh County, Pennsylvania, is a Burr truss with long masonry parapet approaches. This is a regional style used by many builders in the southeastern part of the commonwealth.

Offutt's Ford Bridge in Rush County, Indiana, was built in 1884 by the Kennedy family.

Shieldstown Bridge, over East Fork White
River in Jackson County, Indiana, was built in
1876 by J. J. Daniels.

Harry Evans Bridge, over Rock Run in Parke County, is another product of famed builder J. A. Britton, and dates from 1908.

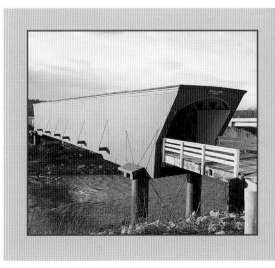

Holliwell Bridge, near Winterset in Madison County, Iowa, has steel caisson piers and a nearly flat roof that are found on several other covered bridges in the area.

Narrows Bridge, over Sugar Creek in Parke County, Indiana, was built in 1882 by J. A. Britton, and is one of the most famous covered bridges in the country. The bridge was replaced (the concrete arch of the new bridge is visible in the photo), but the old bridge is still maintained for foot traffic.

Sulphite Bridge, on the outskirts of Franklin, New Hampshire, is a Pratt truss railroad bridge. It is a deck type bridge, which means the tracks run on the roof. It was once fully covered, as this 1973 photo shows, but it was badly damaged by an arson fire and now sits unhoused.

THE CLASSIC ERA CONTINUES:
BRIDGE COMPANIES AND NEW PATENTS

Big bridge companies that sold structures of iron, and later of steel, offered serious competition to covered bridge builders towards the end of the nineteenth century. England had bridges of iron before America even had any covered bridges, including the world's first major iron bridge, which was over the river Severn at Coalbrookdale in Shropshire (1776–79). In America, the economics were very different. Abundant supplies of cheap large timber meant that wood was the logical choice for bridge material. Inventors tinkered with iron bridges as early as the 1830s, but they did not become widely popular until after the Civil War.

From 1870 onwards, however, the continent was linked by an extensive network of railroads for easy shipment of manufactures, and the market began to change. Iron was still not an instant success. Some designers merely substituted iron parts directly for wood, but iron behaves differently because it lacks wood's elasticity. Failure to understand this difference led to an iron bridge collapse in 1876 that killed 83 people and slowed down acceptance of the new material, but designs created specifically for iron began to win the day.

The great selling feature of the new material was permanence. Americans love to build a grand new structure with fanfare, but regular maintenance later on is another matter. Wooden bridges require some maintenance. Roofing must periodically be replaced, missing side boards must be mended, and accumulated moist dust must be swept from inside or rot will start and the permanence of a covering is lost. Iron and steel seemed almost maintenance free. They were really not because rust turned out to be as severe as rot, and in our day, road salt damage is bringing renewed interest in the use of timber. To many county commissioners or town selectmen in the 1880s, a new iron bridge looked like the smart thing to have.

In most areas, wooden covered bridges were still more economical, except for very long spans, and science offered a means to make them still more thrifty. In 1847, Squire Whipple published the first treatise on mathematical stress analysis. The idea slowly gained acceptance, although it was little noticed at first. Old-time bridge builders had known from experience how large a timber was needed for a given application, and they

The first large-scale iron bridge in the world was built at Coalbrookdale, Shropshire, England, before there were any covered bridges in America. It still exists today.

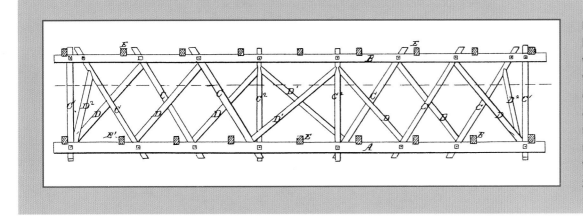

Robert W. Smith's first bridge truss patent was in 1867. The vertical posts in the center were eliminated and several other minor modifications were made, but all Smith trusses follow this general pattern.

tended to err on the side of safety. This meant that many covered bridges were over-designed for the needs of the day. That is why so many have survived, but from the short-term economic point of view, it meant a lot of wasted material. From the 1860s onwards, several inventors addressed this challenge and used the new science to build wooden bridges more cheaply so they could compete with iron.

One of the pioneers, and certainly the most successful, was Robert W. Smith of Tippecanoe City, Ohio, now known as Tipp City. Smith was born in 1833 and was educated mostly at home, but he received a good foundation in geometry. He patented his first bridge truss in 1867, and although there were several later versions, they all followed the same general plan: they had light elongated Xs with no verticals and no iron except for a few bolts. It used wood very efficiently, and seemed too light to support the loads of which we know it is capable. A heavier version doubled some of the web members and was used for longer spans.

As a businessman, Robert W. Smith was as energetic as he was as an inventor. He founded the Smith Bridge Company, which moved to Toledo in 1869. Throughout the 1870s, Smith agents won contract after contract and competed against wood and iron designs. None were built in the Northeast, but from western Pennsylvania through California, they went up by the hundreds. Noted Oregon builder A. S. Miller was the state's franchised agent for the Smith Bridge Company.

Other hopeful inventors followed. Reuben L. Partridge patented a truss in 1872, which was largely inspired by the Smith design, but with interesting metal shoes to make the joints. A few modified examples stand in or near his homeland of Union County, Ohio. Isaac H. Wheeler's 1870 patent has one remaining example in Kentucky. In the excitement, a few builders revived forgotten pre-Civil War plans. Josiah Brown's 1857 truss turned up in Michigan some years later. Horace Childs' 1846 design appeared in the 1880s in Ohio, built by E. S. Sherman, who also patented his own truss of which there are no existing examples. Simeon S. Post's 1863 plan was used several years later

The covered bridge at Cataract Falls in Owen County, Indiana, is a good example of the Smith truss as it was most often built. However, some of the braces are doubled in longer span examples.

The rare Childs truss, patented in 1846, has iron tension rods that take some of the load off the braces. This is the Harshman Bridge in Preble County, Ohio.

in one surviving Indiana bridge. It is an interesting hybrid design. In the Post truss, all the tension members, including the bottom chord, are iron. In fact, the style was chiefly designed as an all-iron bridge. Wood was sometimes used for the compression members as an economy measure, but Post trusses were hardly ever covered.

Among the new inventors, no one was so successful as Robert W. Smith, and even his wooden bridge business declined in the 1880s. By the turn of the twentieth century, steel was definitely in and the use of concrete was just beginning. Covered bridges began to seem old fashioned, although the future still held an unexpected revival.

The bewildering variety in design hides new ways bridge contracts were let in the latter nineteenth century. Smith competed heavily against various descendants of the pre-Civil War firm of Stone & Boomer that specialized in the Howe truss. Both of these corporations were active on a large regional or national level and shipped precut bridge parts from afar by rail. They competed against local builders of the older tradition, some of whom made use of new patents in an effort to remain competitive, while many others, trusted by local officials near home, were still successful with the old styles. Indeed, the conservative Northeast stuck almost exclusively with the old familiar designs of Burr, Town, or Paddleford, built by local craftsmen. Even the Howe truss was uncommon in the Northeast. Brawny James Tasker of New Hampshire was a contemporary of the sophisticated Smith Bridge Company. Tasker was an unusual man, but he highlights the fact that national companies built few covered bridges east of Pittsburgh—except on railroads.

Smith trusses have a distinctive end post framing. The photo shows the former McMillan Bridge in Monroe County, Indiana, that was lost to arson.

The former Myers Bridge in the Dry Brook Valley near Seager, New York, looked like it dated back to the pioneer days, but it was built in 1906–07 by Jerome Moot.

This view was captured from the window of J. J. Daniels' 1867 Mansfield Bridge in Parke County, Indiana. It shows the old mill, which is an important part of the community.

Wood Bridges for the Iron Horse

Railroads used wooden bridges from their earliest days of development. The very first Long truss, designed by the Colonel himself in 1829, was a railroad overpass. Sometimes railroads tried their hand at designing their own special bridge trusses, and they weren't always with happy results. The plans most popular for highway bridges also became the most widely used wooden trusses on railroads—Burr, Town, and Howe.

The Howe truss was designed from the start with trains in mind, and the very first one served a rail line in Warren, Massachusetts, in 1838. Meanwhile, Ithiel Town adapted his truss to rail use with a special double-lattice variety. Lewis Wernwag, the early turnpike bridge builder, lived long enough to construct bridges for railroads. One of his served Harpers Ferry and was blown up early in the Civil War.

A successful design specifically created for railroad use was the McCallum Inflexible Arched Truss that Daniel C. McCallum developed for the Erie Railroad, and patented in 1851. The Erie had previously had bad luck with its special designs, but this one was exceptionally sturdy. McCallum addressed the challenge of pre-stressing, which is why his truss was called inflexible. It had no iron except for bolts and a few special fittings, and it even held up to train wrecks and heavy flood damage. The inventor went on to construct railroads for the Union Army during the Civil War, but his truss fell out of favor because it was difficult to frame.

Covered railroad bridges posed special problems. They were fire-prone, and early locomotives threw plenty of sparks. Railroads hired bridge watchmen to check the structures after every train. Some New England bridges had cupolas on top to let the smoke out, and a few Oregon spans even had water barrels on the roof. The problem persisted until the advent of diesel-electric locomotives, by which time the covered railroad bridge was almost a thing of the past.

This Howe truss covered bridge was built in 1897 to serve a branch line of the Rutland Railroad in East Shoreham, Vermont. The line has been long discontinued, but it once crossed Lake Champlain to Ticonderoga, New York.

Ithiel Town's double lattice truss from the 1835 patent was popular with railroads. It was a competitor to the Howe truss and was still being built in New England into the early twentieth century. This example was built in 1898 in Swanton, Vermont, but was lost to arson in 1987 after it had been abandoned for many years.

Designed primarily for railroads, the McCallum truss was occasionally used for highway bridges. This bridge crosses the Chateauguay River in Powerscourt, Quebec, and is the last existing example of the type, although it has somewhat been modified. The arched top chord is the most distinctive feature.

The magnificent Knight's Ferry Bridge, over Stanislaus River in central California, dates from 1863–64. During its last years in service, traffic was so heavy that it was regulated with traffic lights. The bridge is now retired, but is kept in good condition as an historic monument.

A view inside the Sulphite Bridge near Franklin, New Hampshire, shows the diagonal iron rods and vertical wooden posts of the Pratt truss, which was patented in 1844. This design was rare in covered bridges, but it later became very common as an all-steel truss in a somewhat modified form.

Fisher Bridge, over Lamoille River near
Wolcott, Vermont, is a double Town lattice
truss covered railroad bridge that was built
in 1908. The cupola on the roof was to help
smoke escape and reduce the possibility of
fire from stray sparks.

A second problem of the railroad bridges is that they quickly became obsolete. Covered highway bridges were over designed, but railroads used far more of a bridge's load capacity than highways. As rolling stock became heavier with each passing decade, the earlier bridges were rapidly replaced.

By 1930, there were few covered railroad bridges left. The last concentration of them is in New Hampshire, largely because Jonathan Parker Snow was the bridge engineer for the Boston & Maine Railroad, favored covered wooden trusses, and had them built even after 1900. He was a graduate of the Thayer School of Engineering and carried on a spirited defense of wood construction in an era when it was usually viewed as retrograde. The decline of rail traffic from the 1930s onwards meant that some of these bridges were spared, although nearly all are now unused.

As unlikely as it seems, there were once a few covered aqueducts for canals. They were never common, but Washington, D.C. had a lengthy example over the Potomac.

The Metamora Aqueduct serves the Whitewater Canal in Franklin County, Indiana, and is the country's only surviving roofed canal aqueduct.

The only one that remains serves the old Whitewater Canal at Metamora, Indiana, and dates from 1846, although it was largely rebuilt in the 1940s.

Neglected Little Brother: The Pony Truss

Although the covering made a wooden bridge more expensive to build, it was usually not a difficult matter to add the roof and siding. The trusswork that supported the bridge was already there anyway and formed a long wooden cage. All that was needed for extra framing was a set of rafters, and in most cases, these rested directly on the top chords of the trusses, and then came purlins and shingles. Nailers mounted on the trusses served to hold the side boarding, which was either vertical or horizontal. The siding was sometimes nailed directly to the trusswork, but usually not because it could trap moisture and cause the rot it was supposed to prevent.

Sometimes the trusswork did not reach high enough for a roof. For short spans, trusses only eight feet high or so were sufficient to carry the load. Occasionally, even fairly long spans were built with low trusses. For example, a 126-foot covered bridge in Berks County, Pennsylvania, has half height trusswork because it was built during a timber shortage following a major flood. In such cases, the roofing posed a greater challenge. It required a separate frame either atop or alongside the trusswork to get sufficient overhead clearance for the bridge to be usable.

A half height truss is known as a pony truss, and because of the difficulties, only a few of them were ever fully roofed. They still needed protection from rot, and the common solution was to board in each side of the truss separately, while leaving the top open.

Some early writers on engineering history, accustomed to organizing their thoughts along grand scientific lines of evolution, described these boxed pony trusses as precursors to fully covered bridges. This was a neat concept, but the facts do not support it. Little is known about the dates of the earliest pony trusses, but there is no evidence whatever that they supplied the idea for full weatherboarding. Instead, they were a later development. A few pony trusses were once credited with very early dates, but they were all later structures on early sites where historians confused the replacement bridges with the originals.

The boxed pony truss has long been an unglamorous and neglected structure. No one has any idea how many were built. They lacked the romantic associations of the fully covered bridges even though they shared a common history. They disappeared mostly unnoticed, and only seven remain in North America.

Railroads sometimes used boxed pony trusses for shorter spans. This example still crosses Snyder Brook in Randolph, New Hampshire, although the tracks have been removed.

A passenger train bound for Fitchburg speeds under the former 1908-vintage pony Howe truss in Belmont, Massachusetts, in 1992.

The twin bridges in St. Martins are among New Brunswick's most famous covered bridges. They originally had arched portals, but the entries were squared off by 1976. Outside covered sidewalks have recently been added. The bridges span creeks that flow into a tidewater pool in this active fishing village.

COVERED BRIDGES BY GOVERNMENT PLAN

Even in the late nineteenth century when big bridge companies competed against individual contractors, the decision as to what to build was a local one. County commissioners, or town selectmen in the Northeast, were responsible for the public roads. Each county or town had its own ideas and its own trusted contractors. There was no standardization except on railroads, and every one of those was somewhat different from the next because each line had its own chief bridge engineer.

Railroads took over long distance travel by the Civil War, and the highways served mostly local needs for several decades, but the trend began to shift at the close of the nineteenth century. Bicycles, then automobiles, hit the roads, which were in terrible shape. Roads were muddy in spring and dusty in summer because rubber motive tires caused a different kind of wear on dirt or gravel surfaces than the iron tires and hooves of yesteryear. The public began to demand better roads and a uniform system of posting long distance routes.

The level of government best suited to answer these needs was the state, not the county or town. Shortly after 1900, state governments became widely involved in public road work and created special highway departments between 1910 and 1925.

The automobile caused these new developments, which came at a time when most engineers viewed wood as a material totally outmoded for modern purposes. The volume of auto traffic on local roads was still very light, and the weight of a car or truck was well below the safe load limit of a covered bridge of traditional design, as long as it had been well maintained. Meanwhile, scientific stress analysis made it possible to use wood more efficiently. The new state engineers of several timber rich regions began to take notice.

These lumbering regions were Oregon, Quebec, New Brunswick, and British Columbia. In the first three areas, covered bridges saw an enormous revival once engineers found they could still perform modern tasks at a cost well below that of steel or concrete due to the cheap local supply of timber. In Oregon especially, the steel shortage brought on by World War I turned engineers back to wood. British Columbia built non-covered bridges of creosoted timber instead of covered bridges, but the engineering differences are minor and these bridges are part of the same history.

The government standardization of covered bridge plans in twentieth century Quebec meant that a similar style of bridge could be found from one end of the province to the other. This example stands near Adamsville in the Eastern Townships, but could be found almost anywhere in Quebec's huge territory.

74

Oregon

Covered bridge building began in Oregon in the mid-nineteenth century. Smith Bridge Company agents competed with other builders to span the many rivers and creeks. Bridges from both sources were completely replaced with twentieth century covered bridges in a new era of government standard plans.

The State Highway Commission chose a classic older form, the Howe truss. It was easier to modify for increased strength than the Smith truss. Counterbraces were eliminated towards the ends of the bridge. Rods and braces were better proportioned to the loads they carried. The state provided standard plans around 1918 from a conviction that the counties were being bamboozled by glib bridge company salesmen. Oregon's new government plan covered bridges were part of the reforming spirit of the times.

The counties retained an important say in the overall look of the bridges, except on state highways. The bridges were built by the county engineer. He always worked with a modified Howe truss approved by the State Highway Commission, but he had great discretion in framing details and ornamentation. Sometimes he contracted the work out, but he did not have to do so because he was the boss of a county bridge crew to do the construction.

Oregon shows more variety in its twentieth century covered bridges because even though the state furnished standard plans, they were modified for use by the county engineer. This is the former Meadows Bridge in the midst of the Coast Range mountains in Lane County.

Fisher School Bridge in Lincoln County is another example of the Oregon style. This bridge is a Howe truss, which is used in almost all Oregon covered bridges.

Gilkey Bridge shows the open-sided style favored in Linn County, Oregon. The railroad bridge (left) was once a covered bridge, too.

Linn County first experimented with a wide eaved kind of bridge that had no side boarding. When it was discovered that the unprotected joints at the bottoms of the truss rotted, the county switched to a style with a low boarded sill along the bottom chord and graceful arched portals. The bridges were still light, airy, and answered a common objection to covered bridges, namely that they were dark inside and dangerous for faster traffic.

Lane County was less concerned about dark interiors. Its bridges also often had graceful arched portals, but were weatherboarded almost to the top of the sides. The county later switched to a wider, heavier, boxier style with square portals. All of these were Howe trusses, but they varied in accordance with the preference of the county engineer.

Jackson County tried portal openings with an arch so deep it was almost a semicircle. Douglas County used a variety of styles, including the Cavitt Creek Bridge, with round logs for chords and high pointed portals to allow loaded log trucks. Lincoln County built its Howe trusses with radically flared siding that directed rain runoff far away from the critical bottom chords of the truss. The bridges had graceful arched portals and were painted red. Benton County sometimes used flared siding, but painted the bridges white. Benton County's Irish Bend Bridge was the last covered bridge built in the United States for purely economic reasons in 1954.

The former Brumbaugh Bridge showed the boxy style of the more recent covered bridges that were built in Lane County, Oregon. It was wide enough for two lanes of traffic.

Irish Bend Bridge was the last covered bridge built in the United States for strictly economic reasons. Built in 1954, it crossed an overflow channel of Willamette River in the midst of an agricultural region in Benton County, Oregon. It has since been moved to a park in Corvallis. This view shows the bridge at its original location in 1977.

The beautiful Lake Creek Bridge, built in 1928, is in the Coast Range in Lane County, Oregon.

Oregon built covered bridges in large numbers throughout the 1920s, 1930s, and 1940s. Several went up in the early 1950s. It is difficult to say whether construction stopped due to higher cost of materials because the big timbers were becoming scarce or else because of higher labor costs, increased traffic volume, or just a conviction that such structures had finally passed their prime. Whatever the reason, the construction of covered bridges and modern interstate freeways almost overlapped in time.

Despite their large proportions and recent origins, the covered bridges of Oregon preserve contact with a pioneer past. The Howe truss originally did away with the need for custom framing and introduced manufactured metal angle blocks at the joints. Even

in the old days back east, a Howe truss sometimes went "low-tech" and the parts were produced locally of wood at remote locations, which left only rods and hardware to be imported. This was usually the case in Oregon. Sometimes the blocks themselves were eliminated and the braces were dapped directly into the chords by timber framing methods. In Lane County's Pengra Bridge, built in 1938, the bottom chords are hand-hewn to a length of 126 feet in single sticks, measuring 16 by 18 inches.

In the turnpike era of covered bridges, a designer/builder planned the structure from the start and supervised the construction. In the later turnpike and classic eras, the plan came from a patent file and a contractor adapted it to the site. In the government plan era, a college-trained engineer prepared plans based on patents, which by now

Louis Gravel Bridge, near Sacre-Coeur, Quebec, was a typical colonization bridge. They were originally painted red, but by the time of this 1976 photograph, they were usually gray with green trim. Many of them have been repainted red. The Louis Gravel Bridge still exists, but it has been modified by recent repairs.

79

This structure near Montcerf in the Gatineau Valley is also a typical colonization bridge, or *pont rouge* (red bridge).

A view from the 1932-vintage Cousineau Bridge shows an old barn in Quebec's Gatineau Valley.

were very old, and sometimes sent out a crew of county employees to do the work. Yet abundant virgin timber meant that the men who did the real labor at the job site often used the adze and broadax of the pioneers; no modern sawmill could handle timber of this size. For the bridge crew, the experience was about the same as that of their eastern forebears a century earlier.

Quebec and the Colonization Bridge

Quebec built the most covered bridges in modern times. Its later bridges were mostly the product of the Department of Colonization.

Quebec was already building covered bridges locally in the classic era, and some of them still stand, principally in the Eastern Townships around Sherbrooke. Government plans were available for major structures at an early date since Canada, with a vast expanse of sparsely populated territory, needed major public works whose expense could not be met locally nor completely by private capital. Frederick Preston Rubidge, a government engineer, drew recommended plans for bridges as early as the 1840s, long before the Canadian Confederation of 1867. Iron and steel took over towards the end of the nineteenth century.

Quebec remained primarily agricultural while other regions of North America became industrialized. The new economy of nearby New England provided wages high enough to draw away thousands of farmer's children from Quebec. The province at the

82

time had a very high birth rate, but the long term dream had been to serve in North America as an anchor for a civilization revolving around the French language, the Catholic religion, and an agrarian lifestyle, in opposition to the mercantile urban culture that was developing everywhere else. Emigration threatened Quebec's civilization at its very roots.

The province still had virgin land with agricultural potential, either on the edges of the older parishes or in the more distant wilderness regions. If the emigrants could be

Levasseur Bridge, near Authier-Nord, Quebec, was built in 1928 in the Abitibi region, which was first opened to agricultural settlement around the time of World War I.

THE CURIOUS CASE OF THE COVERED BRIDGE "REPLICA" 1950–1980

People in the eastern United States were surprised that covered bridges were still being built in the 1950s. There, the style had died out at least two generations earlier. Every year, dozens more disappeared to road projects and there were then no official plans to preserve the bridges. Tracking down covered bridges became a challenging new hobby, and enthusiasts formed societies in the 1940s and 1950s to trade notes and work for preservation. Historian Richard Sanders Allen founded the quarterly magazine *Covered Bridge Topics* in 1943, and it is still published today.

Hundreds of people decided that it was not enough to collect photographs of the old relics. They wanted covered bridges of their own. A few individuals with land and resources managed to save covered bridges from the wreckers by moving them onto private property. However, an average covered bridge is larger than a house, so most people found it impossible to own a real one.

Their solution was to construct a small scale replica. The word replica has long been used to describe these structures, although it is not correct. The backyard structures were never accurate reproductions of any old historic bridge. They were very small in scale, and the vast majority lacked functional trusswork. Ordinary dimension lumber was sufficient to hold them up. Since they were usually for foot traffic only, they were often narrower than they were tall. They had no relation to the historic covered bridges, but they indicated the place where covered bridges occupy in American romantic folklore.

Nearly all of these homeowners acted individually. Most seem to have thought that they had just built "the last covered bridge," and local newspapers dutifully wrote them up as such, but they were part of a large-scale movement that swept the

This little covered bridge near Quaker City, Ohio, was privately built but old and authentic. The photo was taken in 1973, but the bridge is long gone.

country. Over 600 of these covered bridge copies appeared in America from about 1950 to 1980. They rivaled the old covered bridges in number, and greatly outnumbered them in many areas such as Massachusetts, Connecticut, New Jersey, Michigan, and Illinois.

Some of the new bridges were built on a grander scale than the backyard copies. Vermont's Quechee Lakes real estate development built a shed on top of an existing concrete bridge in 1970. The result still appears in tourist literature as an example of a quaint New England covered bridge, although there are several real ones not far away. Many other full-scale imitations sprouted on development roads elsewhere. It was not a new idea; imitation covered bridges were suggested for Vermont's Green Mountain Parkway project, which was proposed around 1940, but never built.

The covered bridge copy as folk art was probably innocent enough. Unfortunately, many people saw absolutely no difference between the new copies and the real historic covered bridges, which were still disappearing at a rapid rate. The copies found their way into tourist guidebooks and newspaper reports, and their sheer numbers masked the urgency for preservation of the real ones. There is still much confusion on the subject today, and most publications on covered bridges include at least a few structures of dubious authenticity. New folk art bridges are less commonly built today. A few of the recent examples have used traditional timber framing techniques.

Coldwater Bridge no longer serves the public roads of Calhoun County, Alabama, but it has been moved to a nearby park.

Note the falling rock warning sign at the former Point Wolfe covered bridge in Fundy Park near Alma, New Brunswick. Authorities later blasted the cliff face in an effort to remove the danger, but the rocks fell off and crushed the covered bridge. It was replaced with an all-new covered bridge in 1992.

The former covered bridge near Launay, Quebec, was also in the Abitibi region, which is still a stronghold of covered bridges. This beautiful example is now gone.

encouraged to develop new farms in Quebec's outlying areas, the French agrarian civilization of North America could extend itself and carry into the future.

A few critics at the time, and many more in later decades, thought the growth of cities and an industrial civilization was inevitable. By rejecting such development, the French would leave the new prosperity to others and guarantee their own impoverishment. Critics could not fail to notice that the French agrarianism of their province came largely from an eloquent elite of clerics and of lawyers who did not work the land themselves. Quebec's intellectual leaders of the late nineteenth century were sincere in their beliefs that their special rural civilization was the only force that could preserve religion, art, and culture in the midst of North America's growing commercial and urban society. They enlisted the provincial government to further their ideas, which eventually included covered bridges built to standard plans.

Honore Mercier, Quebec's nationalist premier from 1887 to 1891, created the Department of Colonization to marshal resources in agriculture. He reserved the portfolio for himself, and his subminister, Monsignor Antoine Labelle, was a prominent cleric who had been beating the drum for colonization for years. Government aid for new colonies included roads and bridges, and although Mercier at first favored metal bridges, it became obvious that wooden covered ones would be far more economical.

The first few years of the Quebec government colonization bridge are not well understood. No one knows the name of the engineer who first drew up the standard covered bridge plan that became common in the twentieth century. It first appeared around 1905 and was a streamlined truss that was easy to erect. It was a variant of the Town lattice with refinements so settlers could build their own bridges under a government supervisor without skilled carpenters in the crew. The plan used simple sawn planks produced by local sawmills. Joints were held by metal spikes that could be driven quickly, instead of the older treenails that required boring holes. Wooden cribs filled with loose round stones served for abutments. Private contractors built some of these bridges, but many were built directly by settlers who always followed the standard plans endorsed by a government engineer. There was a plan for boxed pony trusses as well.

The Department of Colonization settled many new parishes in recently opened territories such as Abitibi in the northwest, and also extended the ranges of parishes in the older regions. The covered colonization bridge can be found everywhere in the

Bowman Bridge was one of Quebec's longest covered bridges and measured 433 feet. It crossed the river du Lievre, which was once famous for log drives. Built in 1929, it was arsoned in 1995.

Many covered bridges were built for the Gaspe Circular Highway, or Boulevard Perron, in the 1920s and 1930s, but most were replaced three decades later. The highway made the entire Gaspe region a famous tourist destination. This picturesque scene was at Anse-au-Griffon, near the tip of the peninsula, and was photographed by noted pianist Leo Litwin. *NSPCB Archives*

province, even mixed among the older classic era covered bridges of the Eastern Townships. The prosperity of the 1920s brought large scale industry to Quebec and the new jobs began to siphon off the supply of settlers, but the Great Depression sent them back to the land in huge numbers. Dozens of new settlements with their colonization bridges appeared throughout the 1930s and into the 1940s.

The last new agricultural colony was founded in 1948. The flow of settlers continued into the 1950s, but it slowed to a trickle as the world of industry and commerce won the long economic battle and a new generation of intellectuals questioned the wisdom of opening new lands in the first place. The Department of Colonization struggled on, and in a few places, it contracted networks of roads and covered bridges to be built in advance for settlers who never came.

Quebec's last covered bridges date from the mid-1950s, the same period when the style died out in Oregon. Their place in history is unique. Covered bridges everywhere are tangible symbols of an older civilization built in wood and based on agriculture, but Quebec's colonization bridges came from a fierce, organized, intellectual effort to maintain such a civilization against the pressures of modernism. The province today is an entirely different place, but the bridges remain as a testimony to a surprisingly recent past.

New Brunswick and British Columbia

New Brunswick is the third region where covered bridge construction survived into the 1950s, and one was built as recently as 1958. Colonization projects inspired some of them, but most served local roads in established older regions. The Public Works Office at Fredericton provided standard plans in very specific detail around 1900, such as that the angle blocks at Howe truss joints were to be made of hackmatack. Local contractors usually did the construction work, rather than government employees or crews of settlers.

New Brunswick bridges most often used the Howe truss, but sometimes a local design was used that went loosely under the name of Burr. It was a distant development of the old Burr truss, but with flared posts. Instead of an arch, it had long extra diagonal braces that spanned several panels near the ends where the load is concentrated. In spite of the work of the later nineteenth century inventors, the covered bridge trusses that were built in North America in the government plan era were the three most popular older plans: Howe (easy to revamp in stronger form and adjustable); Town (easy to build); and Burr. New Brunswick's Burr truss was intricate and required great skill to frame. Its survival in the region can only be explained by stubborn local tradition, and some local engineers believed it to be stronger than the Howe truss.

Heppell Bridge crosses Matapedia River near Causapscal in the western area of the Gaspe Peninsula. Note the beautiful French barn in the background in this photograph from 1976.

89

Through a geographical technicality, this little covered bridge near Val-Paradis, Quebec, is now in the far-north municipality of James Bay. It was built in 1954 towards the end of the colonization bridge era.

Many New Brunswick timber trusses were built without a roof and sides, but they usually used the same truss styles as covered bridges. Here, the former McLean Bridge in Kent County shows the province's Burr truss variant. Built in 1958, it was used for 40 years.

New Brunswick came up with the hip roof, a special refinement in covered bridge housing. Such treatment is known in Switzerland, but it is very rare in America, and no one knows what influence came to bear in New Brunswick. Old Acadian houses sometimes had half-hip roofs, and that may have been the origin of the style. The older covered bridges were more likely to have hip roofs than the newer ones, but they appeared on both Burr and Howe trusses.

Around 1930, provincial engineers decided that covered bridges, with their dark interiors, were unsuited for major roads, but timber structures were still more economical at the time. The solution was to build non-housed wooden trusses in places with heavy traffic or visibility problems, while the quiet side roads had covered bridges. The new open bridges sometimes used the Howe plan and sometimes the Burr, but yet another Burr variant came from the government drawing boards for open bridges. It had graceful arches that swept up and over the top chords of the trusses. Trestle approaches included elegant concrete railings that imitated the arch form of the main wooden spans.

This plain-looking bridge in a beautiful setting was a typical scene of New Brunswick in bygone decades. The structure still crosses Kennebecasis River near Sussex in Kings County, but it has been bypassed since this photograph, circa 1976.

The former Bell Bridge was also in Kings County, which is known as the covered bridge capital of New Brunswick.

The Tranton Bridge, near Sussex, is one of the many covered bridges still standing in Kings County, New Brunswick. This is how it looked in 1976.

British Columbia built Howe trusses until 1961, but they were never covered. There, provincial engineers preferred to creosote their timbers and sometimes protected the top chords with sheet-metal coverings. These structures were long-lasting, but not as durable as well-maintained covered bridges. The preservative treatment could not penetrate the timbers deeply, so they could still rot inside if water got in through cracks in the wood, or where the ends were cut for joints. A few dozen of these bridges remain, but they are slowly being replaced. An old engineering treatise makes a tantalizing reference to steel pipes in British Columbia construction, which suggests the use of modernized Town lattice trusses, but if any were ever built, they haven't come to light. The province once had a few large railroad bridges whose sides were boxed in separately. They were sometimes called covered bridges even though they lacked a roof; one remains near Keremeos, and was converted to highway use.

The Peter Jonah Bridge in Albert County, New Brunswick, demonstrates the unusual hip roof style found on some New Brunswick covered bridges.

A five-span, non-housed Howe truss crossed Fraser River in Quesnel, British Columbia.

The longest covered bridge in the world stretches 1,282 feet in seven spans across the Saint John River in Hartland, New Brunswick. The province once had several other covered bridges in the 600 to 900 foot range, but this is the last one that is left. It once served the Trans-Canada Highway and has been preserved for local use. A sidewalk has been added since Raymond Brainerd took this photograph in 1938. *NSPCB Archives*

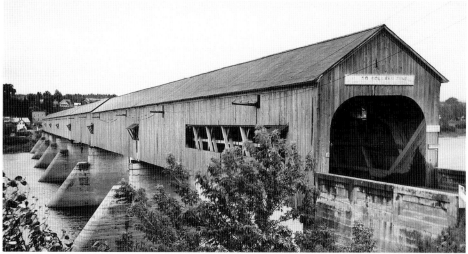

The Ashnola River Road Bridge crosses the Similkameen River near Keremeos, British Columbia. Although it doesn't have a complete roof, it is sometimes called a covered bridge. It has been converted for highway use, but was originally a railroad bridge. A smaller and similar structure still exists in Washington state, and there were once a few others scattered across the Northwest.

New Hampshire's Bath Bridge, built in 1832, is still in daily service.
A very old general store (left) is also popular with tourists.

3.8 m

MAXIMUM
10 t

PRESERVATION AND REVIVAL

Historic preservation is a matter of national interest, but local action. Several national or regional covered bridge societies appeared on the scene from the 1940s and onward. One Ohio group, which today is known as the Ohio Historic Bridge Association, bought a covered bridge in 1960. For a long time, the preservation battle was all uphill. Some creative activists in Lancaster County, Pennsylvania, brought billy goats to guard a threatened bridge in 1961. The structure was named the Eden Bridge and the goats wore signs warning, "Commiss'ners Keep Off." The bridge was replaced anyway.

By 1970, the tide began to turn. The bridges were important to tourism. Lancaster County switched whole-heartedly to preservation after the floods from Hurricane Agnes in 1972 destroyed several historic bridges. Today it is somewhat rare for a covered bridge to be replaced for highway improvements.

In some ways, the preservation challenge has become more complicated. An early solution was to bypass a threatened bridge, which buys time, but this has often proved an unwise practice. Covered bridges do need regular maintenance, but if they have not had repairs for a long time, they may need expensive work. While they continue to be used, highway funds can be used for repairs.

In some cases, federal bridge standards for loads and clearance may complicate the issue, but if bypassed, funding usually becomes much more difficult. Occasional special grants are available, but parks departments and historical societies do not have budgets large enough to fund major restoration if needed. Therefore, bypassed bridges often get neglected, and the longer the neglect continues, the more expensive the repairs become. Some bridges have been lost this way.

It is better to keep covered bridges open wherever possible. Alternate access routes may be an issue if tall trucks use the road. Many bridge portals have been smashed by drivers who did not heed the warning signs. Special steel height barriers now guard bridge approaches in various locations. When loads are concerned, covered bridges are usually adequate for modern traffic if they have been well maintained, but if they aren't, how should they be repaired?

Today the preservation debate is how to repair covered bridges. Should modern materials such as steel, concrete, or glue-laminated timber be used? Or if traditional timber framing is the method, to what extent should partly decayed members be replaced completely with new timber? To what extent should they be repaired with only short added pieces of new material? Is cosmetic appearance important, or should the highest priority go to preservation of the most possible historic structural timber?

An easy repair is to stick a pair of steel beams under the entire bridge. The side view is ruined, but the old structure remains intact for a future, more enlightened restoration. A second and more common solution is to remove the entire floor while leaving all the

The remains of a demolished covered bridge sat in a field near Saint-Valerien, Quebec, in 1976. The Transports Ministry is now much more committed to saving covered bridges, thanks to dedicated work by preservationist Gerald Arbour and others.

trusswork intact, then hide steel beams inside where the old floor was. This saves the side view, but it is less satisfactory from the preservationists' view. The old style of floor framing could be rebuilt in the future without major effort. Stub ends of the old floor beams may even remain to provide dimensions and spacing. The claim is often made that the floor system of many covered bridges is unlikely to be original anyway. This is probably true in the northeastern United States, but it is less certain elsewhere. Engineers with an eye for aesthetics often use a timber plank deck on top of the added steel so the bridges look natural unless you happen to check underneath.

Gregg Bridge, over Wakatomika Creek in Licking County, Ohio, looked like an antique in 1973. It was built with the multiple kingpost truss, which is typical in this region.

99

The lovely covered bridge near New Germantown in Perry County, Pennsylvania, was photographed in 1978.

Another and much more disruptive method of repair is to disassemble the old trusses entirely, then rebuild them using hidden modern materials, such as steel plates or glue-laminated timber. This approach was used in 1989 to strengthen the longest covered bridge in the United States, a two-span structure over the Connecticut River between Windsor, Vermont, and Cornish, New Hampshire. The job posed clear-cut preservation questions, and since the two towns and states involved had different views on the subject, it generated much discussion and publicity.

The Windsor-Cornish Bridge was built in 1866 and used an experimental modification of the Town lattice truss, with slightly notched square timbers instead of flat planks. The historical literature has given disproportionate attention to this interesting, but rare modification. It seemed like a promising idea, and it worked well in bridges of shorter span. Here the two spans were each a little over 200 feet long. It turned out that notched square timbers, held at some of the joints with a bolt, pivoted more than flat

100

planks held at every joint with two or more fat treenails. This caused the bridge to sag at an early date. There was never any question about safety, and the Windsor-Cornish Bridge successfully saw more than a century of heavy service. Eventually ice jams caused damage by knocking at the bottoms of the trusses, and by the 1980s the bridge needed major work.

The National Society for the Preservation of Covered Bridges, through its special consultant David W. Wright (who today is the society's president), was in favor of nineteenth century preservation methods. The traditional technique of adding laminated arches would have brought the bridge up to a high load capacity and saved all the original trusswork. From the preservationists' standpoint, this was the ideal solution, but the bridge was barely wide enough for two-way traffic. If the laminated arches were placed inside as usual, they would constrict the passage. At 160 feet in total length, a one-lane bridge would have been unthinkable between Windsor and Cornish. It was

A view inside the New Germantown Bridge shows that it is a hybrid style that combines a multiple kingpost truss with queenpost style bracing instead of an arch.

Waggoner's Bridge, also in Perry County, has been closed since this 1977 photograph was taken, and is now in poor condition.

technically feasible to place the arches outside the trusses, but this would change the exterior appearance. After much discussion, engineers rejected the arch plan. Instead, they discarded much of the original trusswork and added hidden modern materials.

Despite the loss of much of the historic trusswork, Windsor-Cornish Bridge received an award for preservation excellence and is looked on with favor by most engineers. It highlights a serious challenge that bridge preservationists always face, namely the prejudice for the new, which thoroughly permeates engineering culture. It requires high intelligence to be an engineer, yet the people are not immune to fads. The culture nearly always favors the new and innovative. You won't get attention doing things as they were

102

The site of this covered bridge near Beaver Springs in Snyder County, Pennsylvania, was inundated by a new reservoir, but the bridge was moved to a nearby park.

done in the past, even when this works perfectly. It is possible to restore covered bridges by entirely traditional techniques, but most engineers do not trust this way and are not prepared for it by their professional training.

Another preservation approach is to replace all decayed timbers with new ones of the same kind. This was not possible in the Windsor-Cornish case, but often is elsewhere. Some favor the replacement of entire timbers, even when only a part is decayed, on the theory that it produces a neater looking bridge and preserves the stress path of the original truss design. This approach may lead to the majority of timber being replaced so there is little historical material left. Preservationists generally favor "sistering," which means the addition of short extra members to do the job of the decayed area, while preserving as much old timber as possible. In several recent cases in Vermont and Kentucky, old covered bridges have been completely demolished and replaced with new wood.

On occasion, change may be justified if the bridge has an original design defect. Perrine's Bridge in Rifton, New York, is famous to northbound travelers on the New York

The abandoned Kesler Bridge on the Banks-Franklin county line in Georgia is now gone.

Eakin Mill Bridge, just off the Appalachian Highway in Vinton County, Ohio, was closed for many years, but it has recently been repaired.

State Thruway, which was rerouted to save the bridge. The siding did not extend low
enough to cover the ends of the Burr arches, which had badly rotted by 1969. An accurate
restoration was done that year, but it repeated the design flaw and gave the chance for
decay to start again. The siding probably should have been extended lower, and old
photographs suggest that it once did.

Another caution involves abutment work. Many covered bridges, especially in New
England, sit on dry laid stone abutments with random courses. These foundations are
difficult to analyze for repair work, although many have held up for over a century. The
temptation is to encase them in concrete, but an interesting and beautiful design feature
is thereby lost. The Hutchins Bridge of Montgomery, Vermont, once used a streamside
outcrop of bedrock for the east abutment and was filled out sparingly with a little extra
stone. All is now hidden behind a huge wall of concrete. This is just one example among
many where old abutments have been lost. There is a great need for specialists in old
stonework, but few have come forward.

Arson is a major challenge to covered bridges that has been very hard to combat.
The problem is not a new one. It goes back to at least the early 1950s. Every year covered
bridges are torched; five were burned in 2002. In very few cases, the fires are kindled
by residents who want a new bridge to allow tall trucks, but the blazes are almost
always set for someone's personal enjoyment. Nearly 200 covered bridges have been
destroyed by arson.

Before the 1980s, arson received very little attention. Everyone hoped the problem
would go away by itself, but it did not. Offenders were rarely ever caught, and if convicted,

they received very light sentences. The problem was national and a few regions lost all or nearly all of their covered bridges to arson sprees.

Arsonists today are more likely to be apprehended thanks to diligent local police work and increased public awareness of the problem. Several covered bridges that were damaged or destroyed have been repaired or rebuilt. In one disheartening case in Maryland during the 1960s, the new covered bridge was burned and was not rebuilt a second time. A number of covered bridges now have dry pipe sprinkler systems or fire alarms. Others include new fire retardant treatments that are easier to apply and do not reduce structural strength. However, no such system is foolproof, and since it is impossible to keep remote sites under constant patrol, we are unfortunately likely to lose more covered bridges to arson in the future.

The former Johnny Little Bridge in Licking County, Ohio, was partially supported by steel beams during its last days.

The long covered bridge over Ammonoosuc River in Bath, New Hampshire, once crossed a railroad line, as well as the river. Train service has since been discontinued and the tracks have been removed.

Milton S. Graton found ingenious ways to support bridges during repair work. On this job in New Hampshire in 1983, he used a temporary suspension system.

Covered Bridge Revival?

Near the hamlet of McKenzie Bridge in Lane County, Oregon, a flood in 1964 took out the covered Belknap Bridge. Local citizens wanted to replace it with another covered bridge, and the county graciously conceded to them. The all new 1966 Belknap Bridge looks as if the Lane County Engineer pulled plans from the 1940s out of his drawer, but it was designed by a private engineering firm. Linn County, just to the north of Lane County, replaced a failed covered bridge with a new one of similar design in 1966, as well.

These covered bridges, and several others more recently, were not built for strictly economic reasons, so they represent a period of covered bridge history different from before. They were built because citizens liked and demanded covered bridges. These bridges were not backyard imitations, nor sheds to hide a bridge of modern construction. The wooden trusswork carried the live load and was covered to prevent rot.

Both of these Oregon examples replaced previous covered bridges and offered historical continuity in their locales. Two years later, Woodstock, Vermont, went a step further and built

The interior of Bath Bridge in New Hampshire shows a very unusual variant of the Burr truss. It has laminated arches that were later added.

a covered bridge to replace a failing iron structure on Union Street (now named Mountain Avenue). The new bridge was a Town lattice truss, just like the covered bridges of the nineteenth century. Construction began in 1968 and was completed in 1969.

Milton S. Graton built Woodstock's new covered bridge in the manner of a hundred years before. Graton was from Ashland, New Hampshire, and began his career hauling lumber and later went into rigging and contracting. In 1954, he removed the remains of a neglected New Hampshire covered bridge that had fallen into the river. He was impressed at the quality of workmanship in the original construction when he found the old joints had remained so tight the wood inside had not even discolored. Graton found rigging jobs that moved covered bridges. Throughout the 1960s, he specialized in covered bridge repair. He used traditional methods and was the natural choice when Woodstock built an all new covered bridge.

110

Graton was called back to restore his own bridge after a serious arson fire in 1974. (The vandals were apprehended, but received suspended sentences.) He built more new covered bridges in the 1970s and was busy with repair jobs. He died in 1994, but son Arnold and grandson Arnold Jr. still carry on the family business. The Gratons are a three-generation bridge building family, like the Kennedys of Indiana and the Kings of Georgia a century before.

Town lattice trusses are the Gratons' specialty, but they build other plans as requested. A field near the bridge site serves as a work yard, and the whole bridge is usually built on land. The Gratons use their considerable rigging experience to pull the bridge out over the river on falsework. They sometimes use power equipment, but they often use oxen to move the bridge into place.

Hoke's Mill Bridge in Greenbrier County, West Virginia, has been bypassed since this photograph was taken in 1975.

Leatherwood Station Bridge in Parke County, Indiana, was a product of J. A. Britton in 1899. Here it is shown at the original location in 1977. Four years later, it was moved to a nearby historical museum.

Milton Graton was gifted at public speaking and became nationally known when Charles Kurault featured him on a segment of his *On the Road* television show. Son Arnold is a quiet man, but he shares his father's dry Yankee humor. When complimented on the stout bottom chords in a Howe truss he had just built in Lebanon, New Hampshire, Arnold simply remarked, "We used up all the lumber we had on hand."

A new Graton covered bridge or a repair to an old one contains materials and framing techniques that were used in the nineteenth century. There are no hidden steel plates or glue-laminated timbers. When selectmen in one Vermont hill town insisted that Milton Graton add steel beams under a bridge he was repairing, he reluctantly complied. The beams were stored underneath, but the bridge did not quite touch them. Its sturdy restored trusses still supported the floor.

Salisbury Station Bridge over Otter Creek, between Cornwall and Salisbury, Vermont, is about to receive major work. It appears to have been painted yellow with red trim at one time. This photo was taken in 1974.

Haupt's Mill Bridge in Bucks County, Pennsylvania, succumbed to arson in 1985. Like all of the county's covered bridges, it was a Town lattice truss. Most of the other counties in the area preferred the Burr truss.

Graton published his autobiography in 1978 under the title *The Last of the Covered Bridge Builders*. As it turns out, he was not the last, but rather the first of a new breed. The demand for covered bridge repair has brought several other timber craftsmen to the fore. Some do things the traditional way, while others work with some new materials.

Ohio's John Smolen, who was Ashtabula County's engineer for many years, began to reinforce the numerous covered bridges in his charge with various methods. He went on to build four all new bridges. Like an inventor, he experimented with truss types. Smolen built two highly unusual Pratt trusses. A modified variety of Pratt was once very popular for all-steel bridges, but relatively few were ever built with both wood and steel. Ashtabula County had 12 covered bridges in 1980, but has 16 today.

It is interesting to compare American bridge building practice with that of Europe. Switzerland, Germany, and Austria all have large numbers of covered bridges, and occasionally new ones are built. The Swiss particularly prefer ultra-modern prefabricated timber construction for their new covered bridges, although they are sometimes housed in a more traditional style. Some of these have replaced very old, heavy timbered, hand-framed

The famed Taftsville Bridge, near Woodstock, Vermont, was built in 1836. It's been repaired various times over the years and is still in heavy daily service.

This long-gone covered bridge over Deerfield River in Charlemont, Massachusetts, was photographed by Raymond Brainerd in 1938. *NSPCB Archives*

bridges. In one startling example, the old covered bridge still stands beside the new bridge. Contrary to the American perception, old architecture is not always preserved from modernization even in Europe.

The wide appeal of covered bridges is hard to define, but the folklore clustered about them is decidedly romantic. They were "kissing bridges" where a couple traveling by buggy could linger unobserved. They were "wishing bridges," for a wish made in the mysterious cool darkness of a covered bridge just had to come true. They are associated with quiet days spent at a favorite fishing spot, or hours spent splashing in the swimming hole. They still fulfill these functions today, but they might recall childhood terrors, for crossing one alone on a moonless night was an experience long to be remembered.

Covered bridges once had their own distinctive smell; a blend of hay and old wood, with perhaps the occasional pungent whiff of horse manure. Decades of automobile travel have left the bridges odorless, but the occasional back-country bridge still tickles the nose with the sweet aroma of yesteryear.

With so many pleasant associations and a sense of the depth of history, there is no doubt about the appeal of covered bridges. It is best to see them well maintained, but even when they are not, they offer what architect Lee H. Nelson once called "the quintessence of romantic dilapidation."

Several covered bridges in Kentucky have been torn down and replaced with all-new covered bridges. Such a fate awaited the Goddard Bridge in Fleming County, but local preservationists protested and the old bridge will be repaired.

Hutchins Bridge in Montgomery, Vermont, formerly used a streamside rock outcropping for an abutment, which is now hidden behind a huge wall of concrete.

Auchumpkee Creek Bridge in Upson County, Georgia, was completely destroyed by a flood and could not be salvaged. It was later replaced with an entirely new covered bridge built by Arnold Graton, son of Milton S. Graton.

McBride Bridge in Madison County, Iowa, was lost to arson in 1983. It had the nearly flat roof that is found on other covered bridges in this county.

Brinton's Bridge over historic Brandywine Creek, near Chadds Ford in Chester County, Pennsylvania, was lost to arson in 1957 and was never replaced. Note the stepped false front portals that were sometimes found on covered bridges in this region. *Herbert Richter, NSPCB Archives*

Keefer Station Bridge in Northumberland County, Pennsylvania, is still there, but it has been the target of repeated vandalism since this photograph was taken in 1978.

The Danley Bridge is set against the lovely
Appalachian landscape of Washington
County, which is in the southwestern corner
of Pennsylvania.

Tynemouth Creek Bridge stands near the Bay of Fundy shore in Saint John County, New Brunswick. This is how it looked in 1976.

Greisemer's Mill Bridge brightens the landscape of Berks County, Pennsylvania, on an early spring day in 1978.

Old circus posters increased the appeal of this covered bridge in Montgomery, Vermont.

More old advertising posters were found on the Poland Bridge in Cambridge Junction, Vermont.

Book's Bridge enjoys a quiet setting over Shermans Creek in Perry County, Pennsylvania.

There are three covered bridges named Jackson's Mill in Pennsylvania. This one is in Bedford County.

Elizabethton, Tennessee, has the only covered bridge in the United States with a hip roof. There are several in the province of New Brunswick, Canada.

Lovely Indiana farmland forms the view from inside McAllister Bridge in Parke County.

The well-maintained Union Bridge over Elk Fork Salt River is one of four covered bridges in Missouri. It is located southwest of Paris in Monroe County.

South Hill Bridge crossed Brouillettes Creek in Vermillion County, Indiana. It was built in 1879 by J. J. Daniels. Its original location was on a rural road paved with red brick. The bridge still exists, but has been moved to a nearby golf course.

The former Fernmount Bridge crossed the Burpee Mill Stream in a remote area of Sunbury County, New Brunswick.

This is how the Hectorville Bridge in Montgomery, Vermont, looked to photographer Raymond Brainerd in 1941. *NSPCB Archives*